Hundreds of nearly talented authors have made staggering fortunes peddling this kind of ultratrendy Gee-whiz- pseudotheraputic-optimism-lite-ology to an audience desperate for validation and self-forgiveness.

Sadly, I am not one of them.

Instead, this book offers a stern dose of reality, in the hope that at least four or more readers have the digestive fortitude and complete lack of financial wisdom to plunk down a few extraneous bucks for the following torrent of unadulterated despair.

Of course, in keeping with the philosophy of this book, I will inevitably be proven wrong…

TO
ERR S. HUMAN

All Rights Reserved.
Copyright © 2020 by Vin Morreale, Jr.

Chicken Fat for the Damaged Psyche

365 Deeply Disturbing Insights Into All That's Wrong With Your World

By

Nevada Blue Piccoletti & Vin Morreale, Jr.

Illustrations and Cover Design by Aaron Coleman

ISBN 978-0-9991473-3-7

academyartspress.com

YOU ARE
SPECIAL!

LIFE IS FULL OF
HOPE AND PROMISE!

THE WORLD
REVOLVES AROUND
YOU!

Vin Morreale, Jr.

True love dies.

Illusions seldom do.

Chicken Fat for the Damaged Psyche

Of course, you are misunderstood. Most people find you completely incomprehensible.

Vin Morreale, Jr.

**Look into the eyes of the elderly and you will see the stunned impact of decades that somehow disappeared in a heartbeat.
The shadow of that confusion will soon be visible in your eyes as well.**

Chicken Fat for the Damaged Psyche

We are seldom as clever as we think...

...or as blameless as we hope.

Vin Morreale, Jr.

The children you love, comfort, protect, support and nurture will one day consider you more annoying than acne.

A few things you can count on...

You will die, as will everyone

you have ever loved or ever met.

Some of them will suffer needlessly.

The sun will eventually burn out, destroying all life on this planet.

But it will not do so before

you have been forced to pay off the staggering slag heap of debt you owe.

Vin Morreale, Jr.

No matter how much you try to pretend, you know in your heart that self-indulgence is not a virtue.

Chicken Fat for the Damaged Psyche

Reality is the world's way of laughing at your goals. Puberty is the world's way Of laughing at your self-image.

Vin Morreale, Jr.

There is a perfect someone out there for everyone. Unfortunately, yours may be living in Alaska and probably smells like month-old fish.

Chicken Fat for the Damaged Psyche

**Life will dwindle
as it must
Leaving dreams
leaving dust.
Wretched or worthy
none to save.
All are brothers
of the grave.**

Vin Morreale, Jr.

We don't always believe what we hear. It's much more comfortable to only hear what we already believe.

Take time for
the little things in life.

The big things are
probably way beyond you.

Vin Morreale, Jr.

It is better to give guilt than to receive it.

In your life, you have made many serious mistakes. Often pretended to be something you were not. Occasionally led others to believe you deserved credit for someone else's work. Disappointed those who trusted you most and couldn't stop yourself from doing something cruel to someone you claimed to care about.

I don't even know you, but I feel pretty confident in making that statement.

Vin Morreale, Jr.

**Everyone is dishonest.
And everyone lies
about not being so.**

Chicken Fat for the Damaged Psyche

Sorry, but there is nothing noble about resisting the tyranny of self-control.

Vin Morreale, Jr.

Gravity grabs speeding planets and prevents them from careening off into space. It holds gigantic buildings, restrains massive oceans, and pins mighty elephants to the ground.

So what chance do you think you have fighting wrinkles?

Chicken Fat for the Damaged Psyche

If only you had more courage!

How different your life might have been!

Vin Morreale, Jr.

We are merely the froth on a river of generations. The past sweeps us up to the churning surface, where we bob along for an instant, sputter, then dissolve. The mighty surge continues long after we are mere mist and memory. In this great flow of humanity, we are a barely noticed ripple in the current. We cannot even claim the surface we occupy for so brief a moment. Yet, we boast and brag, toil and hoard; living out our days as if we owned the entire river.

Life is not about finding yourself.

It is the systematic unraveling of your most jealously guarded delusions.

Vin Morreale, Jr.

Get over yourself.

Everyone else has.

Chicken Fat for the Damaged Psyche

Wisdom does not always come with age

We just get a whole lot better at hiding our mistakes.

Vin Morreale, Jr.

Your body is constantly emitting a barrage of different odors, not all of them pleasant.

You have grown so accustomed to your own smorgasbord of smells, you have lost the ability to judge how offensive they really are.

But don't worry.

Others know.

The hardest thing in life to forgive is blamelessness in others.

Vin Morreale, Jr.

Three people will lie to you every week of your life.

Chicken Fat for the Damaged Psyche

Why is it so difficult for you to let go of the very things you try so hard to push away?

Vin Morreale, Jr.

Go the way

Of fools before you

Losing all

To increase worth

Too soon

The final tally finds you

Richly rotting

Under earth

Chicken Fat for the Damaged Psyche

You will never be the person your parents hoped you would be.

Or the person your children once thought you were.

Vin Morreale, Jr.

Time Is Relative.

If you don't believe it, consider how long each minute seems when spent with relatives over the holidays.

Salmon struggle to swim upstream, only to quickly spawn and die.

Flies dart frantically from one place to another and don't even live a year.

By contrast, majestic oaks never move and survive for centuries.

So why exactly should you ever get up off that couch?

Vin Morreale, Jr.

No matter what they say it will never get better.

You will just become distracted by a continually fluctuating barrage of problems.

Every year, every season sculpts your face and heart. Sometimes gently. Often with far too much enthusiasm.

Vin Morreale, Jr.

**You are long overdue
for a hopeless infatuation or
desperate heartache.**

**You know from the start
it will end badly, but you
just can't help yourself.**

Chicken Fat for the Damaged Psyche

An excess of pride is ugliness internalized.

Vin Morreale, Jr.

Judging by the vast disparity in beauty, health, money, fame and power, it is easy to see that God has his favorites.

It is also pretty obvious you will never be one of them.

You approach most conversations with all the subtlety of an ungreased chainsaw.

Vin Morreale, Jr.

Most hope is Groundless.

Most despair all too justified.

Chicken Fat for the Damaged Psyche

You have broken at least four hearts without ever realizing it.

Simple cowardice has kept you alive this long. But at what cost to your dignity, your future and your soul?

Chicken Fat for the Damaged Psyche

**We are the most agile
at turning away
from our own flaws.**

Vin Morreale, Jr.

To most people you meet you are either an annoyance, a disappointment, a joke or a job.

They say that the meek
shall inherit the earth.
But don't worry,
the lawyers will find some way to
cheat them out of it.

Vin Morreale, Jr.

You have never given the last word to those who truly deserve it.

We are only mostly fashioned
of goodness and virtue.

Yet that unfinished quarter,
where evil hungers and darkness
dwells, there crouches the beast that
during our moments of fear, envy or
embarrassment, tears forth even on
those we love or claim to protect.
A savage side that will, in a
sudden flash of claws,
undo a century of civilization,
a lifetime of kindness.

Vin Morreale, Jr.

Failing memory and blind denial are all that keep you from wallowing in a suffocating, and richly deserved morass of emptiness, regret and despair.

**Finding true love
is no more difficult than
counting the stars in
the noonday sun.**

A surprising percentage of those you regularly fantasize about having herpes, genital warts, or some other highly contagious, sexually transmitted diseases.

Chicken Fat for the Damaged Psyche

We are never half as smart, or nearly as generous as we like to think we are.

Vin Morreale, Jr.

Do you have any idea what a small percentage of your thoughts and beliefs are actually your own? (including this one)

All you need is love
Of course, John Lennon was a wildly successful, world-famous, deeply admired, millionaire rock star when he wrote those words.

Vin Morreale, Jr.

Your constant compromises and refusal to stand up for what you claim you believe in have lost the respect of all those you are trying hardest to impress.

What passes for news today is often wave upon wave of noisy irrelevance, stunning stupidity, and the accumulated info-dust of those with almost nothing worthwhile to say.

Vin Morreale, Jr.

The ratio of people who don't want to see you naked to those who do is at least 100,000 to 1.

Chicken Fat for the Damaged Psyche

Nothing in marriage is ever truly forgiven

Vin Morreale, Jr.

Nobody owes you a living!

Nobody owes you fulfillment or happiness.

Nobody really owes you anything at all.

As soon as you accept these facts, you can stop whining, get off your butt, and do something with your life.

As if we needed another excuse to become even more bloatedly self-important...

A corruption of trial lawyers, media hypocrites and craven politicians have sold us the myth that we have a guaranteed right to never, ever be offended.

And that there should be legal action or monetary compensation for any bruising of our fragile feelings.

In this way, they have turned jokes, casual insults or blatant idiocy into crimes of blasphemy against our deified egos.

**Don't fall for it.
We were never meant to take ourselves so seriously.**

Vin Morreale, Jr.

You think they don't know

any of your secrets.

But they do.

Chicken Fat for the Damaged Psyche

We are never as good at parenting as we claim we are...
Nor half as bad as our children will remember us being.

Vin Morreale, Jr.

Sometimes when you cry, it is only for show. How pitiful is that?

Remember the good old days, before people felt compelled to regurgitate every tedious and insignificant detail of their day, their year, or the last to decades onto any poor stranger too polite to cut them off and run? Back when gossip was an embarrassment, not the most lucrative form of journalism in this country. Before personal lives had to become public knowledge, and shame was a whisper, not a social media whine for attention?

Vin Morreale, Jr.

At this very moment, someone is darkly thinking about how you ruined his or her life.

Chicken Fat for the Damaged Psyche

We are all underachievers, knocked backwards each day by the left-right combination of fear and laziness.

Vin Morreale, Jr.

Anyone who believes that maturity comes with age never attended a high school reunion.

Chicken Fat for the Damaged Psyche

Nothing is half as pitiful as people trying to prove that they aren't.

Vin Morreale, Jr.

Seriously...

...what makes you think anyone is interested in your opinions, cares about your problems, or wants to listen to your endless complaints?

Bird flu, swine flu, Ebola, SARS, coronavirus and flesh eating bacteria could all reemerge as candidates for the next worldwide pandemic.

But what if they were to merge into one highly contagious, hyper-lethal organism?

Just something to think about...

Vin Morreale, Jr.

Two terrible options: Either someone is always watching you... ...or no one ever is.

Never underestimate the corrosive and contagious power of negativity.

Vin Morreale, Jr.

Anything new sagging today?

Chicken Fat for the Damaged Psyche

What pitiable creatures

We mortals be

Who long for love

Yet lose and leave

With wretched regularity

Vin Morreale, Jr.

You have willingly succumbed to the seductive self-mutilation of settling for the least disruptive path in life. What a pity...

Chicken Fat for the Damaged Psyche

We are each and always stalked by stupidity. And it seems to be gaining on us.

Vin Morreale, Jr.

**Live only to accumulate,
and you will be surprised at
how little meaning anything holds
for you in those few
final moments of your life.**

Chicken Fat for the Damaged Psyche

Best dieting tip ever...
Close your eyes and think about how disgusting the entire digestive process really is.

Vin Morreale, Jr.

Dreams of childhood are like your favorite old pair of jeans. Worn, snug and comfortable, but sadly, they will never again fit you like they once did.

Chicken Fat for the Damaged Psyche

You have no idea how many really fun parties you were not invited to this year alone.

Vin Morreale, Jr.

History, literature and love all teach us that genuinely good people simply don't stand a chance in life.

How disheartening it must be to realize that you have absolutely nothing that the tin man, the scarecrow, or the cowardly lion would ever want.

Vin Morreale, Jr.

Nothing succeeds like excuses for failure.

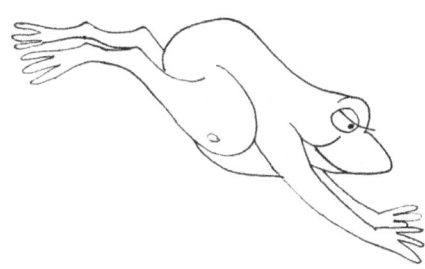

At this very moment...

you could be completely insane and not realize it at all.

Vin Morreale, Jr.

Never Assume Love.
Value it. Seek it. Cherish it.
And cling to it with the ferocity
of a lion and her cub.
But never be foolish enough
to assume it will last.

You have been insincere for so long, you can't even tell where the act ends and the real you begins.

Vin Morreale, Jr.

Some scientists foresee Earth being struck by an asteroid large enough to destroy all civilization. Others point to a new cycle of earthquakes and volcano eruptions sure to cause widespread devastation.

An even larger group believe global warming will throw our planet into chaos.

Meanwhile, you sit back trying to convince yourself that things will be better tomorrow.

Chicken Fat for the Damaged Psyche

If you only knew what they really thought about you...

Vin Morreale, Jr.

The moment your parents die, chunks of your past and your sense of identity evaporates; leaving you feeling there is little left to tether you to the Earth.

**From a larger perspective,
we are all just traveling buffets
for a staggering array of bacteria,
fungi, microbes, viruses and insects
that happily feed on us every
moment of our lives.**

Vin Morreale, Jr.

Nobody Cares

They used to... but your oafish behavior talked them out of it.

Excessive Pride places blinders on our souls, even as it tears up the road map of self-improvement.

Pride peels off our skin and allows us to stalk the earth as raw nerves, cursing every imagined slight to our overly sensitive selves.

But imagine how much worse we would feel without it.

Vin Morreale, Jr.

Great talent is a curse Fortunately, you were never cursed that way.

Chicken Fat for the Damaged Psyche

Life is marked by what we've lost

Knowing not the savage cost

So we turn to hope instead

Which merely mocks us

Once we're dead.

Vin Morreale, Jr.

Jesus was holy, wise and compassionate, and they crucified him for it.

Most of the saints were martyred.

Ghandi, Abraham Lincoln and Martin Luther King were assassinated.

The Pope has to ride in a bulletproof car.

What chance do the rest of us have?

**At this very moment, millions of people are making love.
And you're not.**

Vin Morreale, Jr.

In the long, sad trudge of history, we are each little more than one brief and weary breath exhaled.

Thanks to the wonder of advanced technology, there are dozens, if not hundreds of recorded images of you acting like a total buffoon.

And those humiliating moments will be witnessed by countless others, including your friends, family and potential employers.

Vin Morreale, Jr.

Marriage is the antidote for loneliness. But the side effects can be devastating.

Chicken Fat for the Damaged Psyche

It's okay.

At your age, all that extra weight is understandable.

Vin Morreale, Jr.

No matter what you accomplish, you will never be truly satisfied. No matter how much you have, you will never know contentment.

No matter how much love surrounds you, you will jealously yearn for different smiles, newer arms and other people's joy.

Oblivious to your blessings and always wanting more, you are a study in perpetual incompleteness; a cruel and inescapable prison of your own construction.

Uh-oh...
You've forgotten something terribly important today.

Vin Morreale, Jr.

Those of us not fortunate enough to die young are doomed to perish piece by piece. Our memories slipping away by degrees, dragging with them our independence and the defining elements of our personality.

The withering husks that remain will be less of us and more of some sadly bewildered specter, empty of all but fright and frustrations.

Until this too shall pass…

Chicken Fat for the Damaged Psyche

Pray that you are smart enough to know there are millions upon millions significantly smarter than you.

Vin Morreale, Jr.

Pity the Perfect. Their lives are so unbelievably content.

Chicken Fat for the Damaged Psyche

Your personality repels affection like insect sprays repel mosquitoes.

Vin Morreale, Jr.

All those limitations you allow to rule your life and diminish your destiny... what if they were all fiction, imposed on you by those who had no concept of what you might actually achieve if you were to set your mind to it?

Or even worse, what if all those limitations were both imaginary and self-afflicted?

The most powerful engine known to man is jealousy.

Tell the truth…

You don't really regret a fraction of the things you've done wrong.

You only hate that you feel bad about doing them.

In other words, you regret your conscience more than your behavior.

Console yourself with the thought that there will always be even greater failures than yourself. Although far fewer than you would like to believe.

Vin Morreale, Jr.

**People who say that
'Life is crap' are wrong.
Life is merely the process by which
crap gets dumped on you.**

We build our own prisons, regret by regret, limitation by limitation. Then hide ourselves inside for a life sentence without parole.

Vin Morreale, Jr.

FAILURE FOLLOWS CERTAIN FOOLS

LIKE DARKNESS SWALLOWS LIGHT

EXCUSES, NOT BUT FAILURE'S TOOLS

TO BIND YOU IN ITS MIGHT

Remember The Purpose Driven Life?

It was never about you.

Vin Morreale, Jr.

Polls are based on the false assumption that people actually believe what they are willing to admit to believing.

If that were truly the case, we would not need other people's views to tell us what to believe.

One mistake from deep in your past will always outweigh the thousands of good things you have done since or will ever do.

Proving that goodness is forgettable. And malicious gossip, far too delicious to fade.

Vin Morreale, Jr.

In the beginning, God created light. After which, people created shades, sunglasses, curtains and idiocy.

Chicken Fat for the Damaged Psyche

Dreams are simply the distractions that help reality rob you blind.

Vin Morreale, Jr.

Love is both craving and comfort.

Ache and exhilaration. As much anticipation as fulfillment, it is both knee-quivering need and sigh-induced satisfaction. Equal parts danger, desire, despair and delight.

Each facet must be endured. If we experience happiness without hunger, much of the excitement is lost. That is why one can be comfortably content in a long-term relationship, yet still yearn for the sudden, heart-quickening smile in a stranger's eyes.

Chicken Fat for the Damaged Psyche

Mediocrity in life is earned Every bit as much as success. All you have to do is set your goals ridiculously low, continually question your own abilities, and pretend that your dreams were never really attainable at all.

Vin Morreale, Jr.

Admit it.

You find things charming in strangers you would be horrified to see in your spouse and would absolutely refuse to tolerate in your children.

Chicken Fat for the Damaged Psyche

There's only one thing that everyone on Earth wants...

...and that is MORE.

Vin Morreale, Jr.

Everyone who assured you that "you" could be anything you wanted to "be" was just being kind.

Most things require a level of intelligence, ambition, physical skill, or artistic talent you could never hope to possess.

No matter how kind or noble you are, you are sure to create enemies. A frustrated few who will hate you out of jealousy, baseless paranoia or some perceived slight. There is nothing you can do to appease them. No amends or apology will suffice.

They will take every opportunity to savage your reputation.

And will likely smile while doing it.

Vin Morreale, Jr.

Failure is not an option.

In your case, it is an inevitability.

Once we surrender to suspicion, even the angels are doomed.

Vin Morreale, Jr.

Those lips were never meant for you. For you are not worthy of their sweetness.

Chicken Fat for the Damaged Psyche

There is not a stone, river or piece of ground that was not here eons before you and will not survive you for millennia to come. The home you treasure will either crumble to dust or be owned by others months after you cease to be. Anything you worked so hard for, along with everything you created, will pass to other hands, who will happily claim them as their own property, their work and their ideas.

Vin Morreale, Jr.

In your case, it is probably best not to mix people with pleasure.

Chicken Fat for the Damaged Psyche

Some are born great. Some have greatness thrust upon them. And some, like you, will never rise above the lowest level of competency.

Vin Morreale, Jr.

Debt is a villain forever lurking in the shadows. Too often, we eagerly invite him in, instead of working just a bit harder to keep him out.

Hundreds of thousands of our bravest young men and women sacrificed their time, their families and even their lives so you can enjoy the blessings of freedom.
And you waste it watching reruns.

Vin Morreale, Jr.

A bad temper is like a full bladder. Best held in public, even though it can feel so damned good to let it out once in a while.

How many wonderful memories have you forgotten, while you endlessly obsess over the petty, ugly and totally inconsequential details of your day?

Vin Morreale, Jr.

Our words and actions are little droplets of influence that we shed blindly and scatter about. They fall on those we meet and a few we don't.

Some droplets moisten, drench or drown, while others may evaporate before they are even noticed. It is not for us to know all who are affected by what we say and do. That would be a cruel responsibility indeed.

No dream worth having is ever entirely realistic. If it is, then your dream is too small.

Vin Morreale, Jr.

There is only one thing you do much better than you used to… Wrinkle.

Chicken Fat for the Damaged Psyche

**Trust no one.
Especially those who
ask for your trust.**

Vin Morreale, Jr.

We never really want people to guess our age.

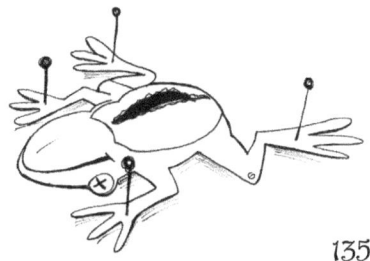

Chicken Fat for the Damaged Psyche

You have lived so long in a state of chaos that you have easily met the state residency requirement.

Vin Morreale, Jr.

Nothing kills progress like contentment. After all, if bacteria were happy, we would not be here today.

**You are definitely part of
the "IN" crowd:
Invisible, Insignificant
..and utterly Inconsequential.**

Vin Morreale, Jr.

In the end, all we can truly own are the delusions we cling to so desperately.

For those who see the world as gentle and nurturing, consider the thick and slimy NASAL LEECH. This slug-like creature infests rivers, streams and lakes around the world, with the sole mission of leaping unseen up the noses of animals, swimmers or people who simply splash their face with fresh water. Its sharp teeth and suctioning jaws burrow through flesh, allowing the leech to engorge itself on the blood of its victims. Because it secretes a natural antiseptic to numb the wound, the 5-inch creature can feed on your insides for months or even years without you noticing. Aside from unexplained nosebleeds, you may not know you have a parasite crawling through sinuses until the day its fleshy brown head peeks out from your nostril, causing those around you to shriek in horror or retch in disgust. Oh, and the slimy bloodsucker can only be wrestled out of your nose with a sturdy pair of pliers just before he ducks his head in and once again hides in your nose.

Vin Morreale, Jr.

You know you are officially old when you shrink from 'too much' excitement and rename boredom as relaxation.

Chicken Fat for the Damaged Psyche

What if your only real purpose in life was cosmic amusement?

Vin Morreale, Jr.

All communication can be mistranslated by jealousy.

Chicken Fat for the Damaged Psyche

Lies come far too easy for you.

Many of those you claim to be close to See only the fiction you have wrapped around yourself like desperate armor.

But you cannot fault them for their mistake. For you have taught them to love only this illusion of you, afraid they would be horrified to learn it bears so little resemblance to the shallow, conscienceless creature you truly are.

Vin Morreale, Jr.

One thing we will never suffer from is a shortage of stupid people.

Chicken Fat for the Damaged Psyche

We are all afflicted and infected

Battered, spattered and rejected

There are no limits to our pains

It's just life's little hurricanes

Vin Morreale, Jr.

It is only the closing curtain that puts the whole drama of your life in perspective.

We hurtle daily towards our inescapable final act, trying to fill it with as much passion and intensity as we can before the lights inevitably dim. But dim they must, and none of us will be there to take a bow or hear the critic's final review.

Chicken Fat for the Damaged Psyche

Don't take it so hard. Some people were never meant to be fulfilled.

Vin Morreale, Jr.

The one thing politicians and military experts agree on is that a nuclear, chemical or biological attack on our homeland is likely unavoidable.

Have a nice day!

Chicken Fat for the Damaged Psyche

You have spent far more time agonizing over the meaning of life than rising up and attempting anything that might give your life some meaning.

Vin Morreale, Jr.

We watch soap operas to see rich and beautiful people become more miserable than ourselves.

But this is fiction. In real life, they will always have beautiful children, enjoy luxuries we will never know and be pretty damn happy about it.

Chicken Fat for the Damaged Psyche

You have broken far more promises than you have kept.

Vin Morreale, Jr.

Nobody knows everything. Least of all those who believe they do.

It is a scientific fact that women never spend as much time dressing up and putting on make-up as when they are about to meet an old flame.

The amount of time and energy spent in this beautification process is directly proportional to the degree of anger present when they broke up.

Vin Morreale, Jr.

In older people, maturity often calcifies into extreme crabbiness, which can be as endearing as wrinkles and hemorrhoids.

Chicken Fat for the Damaged Psyche

You have squandered so much precious time hungering for either numbness or oblivion.

And one day you will get your wish.

Vin Morreale, Jr.

The only way most people will forgive your sins is if you achieve vast fame and impossible success. Short of that, you are doomed.

Chicken Fat for the Damaged Psyche

**Love is all you need.
But truthfully, lust is
all you really want.**

Vin Morreale, Jr.

We have so many weapons to wield against those we hate. But for those we love, Guilt is often our weapon of choice.

Your greatest talent is being ignored. Of course, few will ever really notice your gift.

Vin Morreale, Jr.

Relationships don't collapse suddenly. They are deconstructed, insult by insult, recrimination by recrimination.

Chicken Fat for the Damaged Psyche

Your parents always knew you were lying to them.

Vin Morreale, Jr.

We are each given a handful of decades on this earth. A smattering of years, rich or lean, from which we must discover some code of honor by which to live and be remembered.

This is our legacy; not simply that we have lived, but that we have worked to add depth and value and to the painfully brief time we are here.

Chicken Fat for the Damaged Psyche

There are a surprising number of people who wish you were never born.

Vin Morreale, Jr.

It is a foolish dream that we will one day wipe out every disease. Viruses survive by making us ill. And there will always be trillions more of them than there are of us.

Chicken Fat for the Damaged Psyche

You have traded the hard edge of conviction for an invisible, amorphous membrane pliable enough to offend no one.

As such, you have completely misinterpreted what it means to be a grown up.

Vin Morreale, Jr.

Self-interest is the human condition, and betrayal, its cruelest face.

We will all experience the emotional knife in the back, offering only a whimpering, 'how could you?' And knowingly or not, we will all betray another at some point, then find a convenient way to rationalize it as 'all we could have done,' even as we digest the unappealing taste of guilt.

**You will never get everything you feel you deserve.
But then again, you never really deserved even a portion of what you believe you are owed.**

Vin Morreale, Jr.

Young people wear their accomplishments like a badge. Older people squeeze them into a shameless justification to ramble on endlessly.

Chicken Fat for the Damaged Psyche

Love is sure to ravage you

Prey on your hopes

And savage you

And here you willingly remain

Thirsting for its cruel refrain

Vin Morreale, Jr.

Have you ever noticed how hard you have to struggle to be kind, yet how easy it is to lapse into selfishness and careless cruelty?

Too many of us waste our days passing time, passing through, or passing out... surprised we have accomplished so little before we inevitably pass away.

Vin Morreale, Jr.

There is no such thing as NORMAL Even if there was, it would bear very little resemblance to you.

Remember when you were a child, awash in innocence and idealism? Believing that you were put on this earth to accomplish something great, something memorable, something with a lasting benefit to mankind?

How's that working out for you?

Vin Morreale, Jr.

**Advertising assumes we are all dull, easily swayed, and totally without our own opinions.
Which is why it is so effective.**

Chicken Fat for the Damaged Psyche

Waves of sudden misery await you.

Even when everything seems to be going well, it hovers over your left shoulder. Lingering in the background of your fears.
Waiting for the precise moment you fool yourself into believing that it can be avoided.

And then a fog of pain and agony descends to prove you wrong.

So terribly, terribly wrong.

Vin Morreale, Jr.

All seduction happens in the wink of an eye. The rest is merely follow-through.

Chicken Fat for the Damaged Psyche

Oh, well...

Maybe you are just not

the kind for kindness.

Vin Morreale, Jr.

Memories are not facts, but evolving narratives. Each time we pull one out, sharp with truth, we subtly round the corners to more comfortably fit our current worldview, reinterpreting ourselves as either more victor or victim. After repeated retrievals, we have smoothed the memory into an easily handled story we feel comfortable telling over and over, never admitting, or perhaps even realizing, to what degree we have reshaped and disfigured the truth.

How much more time have you spent feeding your ego, instead of nourishing your soul?

Vin Morreale, Jr.

You have trillions of microbes inside your body that survive by feeding on you in continuous small, gnawing increments.

This is likely the inspiration for our modern tax code.

Insurance companies gamble that you won't die until they are able to squeeze the maximum amount of money from you. Either way, you lose.

Vin Morreale, Jr.

At least one person from deep in your past has torn a picture of you into little pieces.

Even the tallest tree can be riddled with ants and fungus.

Vin Morreale, Jr.

Be honest. What have you done of real consequence this week? This year? This decade?

Despite what we would like to believe, statistics show there have always been far more male geniuses than female geniuses.

Then again, mass murderers and psychopaths are almost always male.

Vin Morreale, Jr.

**Don't believe them.
They have always been laughing at
you, not with you.**

A few more things we can count on:

More hurricanes, cyclical recessions, a failing memory, the death of your favorite pet, and an earthquake that will eventually level California.

Have a nice day!

Vin Morreale, Jr.

Nothing is so joyous as the first blush of true love, the gradual sharing of dreams, or the soft, whispered promises of forever.

Sadly, that is something for others to discover. Not you.

Chicken Fat for the Damaged Psyche

We are never able to understand all the things we consistently choose to overlook.

Vin Morreale, Jr.

Face it. This is all there is. It's probably never going to get any better than this.

Chicken Fat for the Damaged Psyche

One day, in the not-too-distant future, as you gasp for those last few desperate breaths, you will curse yourself for the thousands and thousands of accumulated hours you wasted on video games and TV reruns you had seen a dozen times before.

Don't feel bad.

Lots of people never come close to realizing their true potential.

Chicken Fat for the Damaged Psyche

The worst thing about rudeness is that it's terribly effective. Don't you think so, bonehead?

Vin Morreale, Jr.

**The world is flat!
The sun revolves around the earth!
All illness is caused by demons, or an
imbalance of 'humours' in the body!**

**Think of all the scientific 'facts'
that enlightened people from ages past held
as truth, but which seem
so silly to us now.**

**Then imagine how laughable
our own facts and convictions will
seem to those who look back on us
centuries from now.**

Chicken Fat for the Damaged Psyche

No matter how old you get, your nose and ears will never stop growing.

Vin Morreale, Jr.

**There are dark and twisted sides of your soul that you have never shared with anyone.
It is best that you don't...
for their sanity and for yours.**

Trusting others is the surest way to decimate your hopes and lose almost everything you value. The only thing more heartbreaking is never to trust at all.

Vin Morreale, Jr.

The reason you may find this book amusing, disturbing or depressing is that the anxieties underlying all of these dreads, embarrassments and self-doubts are common to virtually every person you meet. To dispel their nagging grip, you must admit your fallibility, then forgive and maybe even laugh at yourself.

But you won't, will you?

Chicken Fat for the Damaged Psyche

At least once a week, someone walks right by you who could completely change your life. And you never even notice.

Vin Morreale, Jr.

You were right.

There really is less time in the day. The more years that pile up behind you, and the fewer left in your future, allow time to slip by more rapidly.

This is known as the Old Coot's Theory of Relativity.

Chicken Fat for the Damaged Psyche

It doesn't matter how much you have, what you do, or even where you are in life. You just can't seem to make yourself happy.

Vin Morreale, Jr.

The sense of smell is a biological miracle. Hundreds or thousands of particles, no matter how offensive, travel into your nose and are sucked straight into your nasal cavity to be smelled, sampled and then absorbed.

Remember that every time you walk by rotting garbage, visit a restroom or your dog has gas.

Chicken Fat for the Damaged Psyche

**Life is short.
And you have slept through
more than one-third of it.**

Vin Morreale, Jr.

Most of the biggest bores and pompous blowhards are absolutely convinced people are interested in their opinions. What do you think about that?

Chicken Fat for the Damaged Psyche

The biggest problem with excuses is that they almost always work.

Vin Morreale, Jr.

If idiocy was a virtue, you could qualify for sainthood.

You frequently fantasize about being wildly unfaithful.

And even if you never act on those fantasies, you still construct inner arguments to rationalize them, just in case anyone were to get a glimpse of your inner pervert.

Vin Morreale, Jr.

Fossil records show that every thirty-five million years or so, the earth is host to a mass extinction.

It is estimated that 99% of all species that ever walked, flew, swam or slithered on this planet have already disappeared forever. And the clock is ticking on us.

Chicken Fat for the Damaged Psyche

Ask any parent...

Nothing humbles the heart like raising teenagers.

Vin Morreale, Jr.

**You have always envied those with deeper faith.
And they pity or despise you in return.**

All human societies are inherently primitive. What we choose to define as Civilization is merely a matter of degrees. If you don't believe that, try cutting someone off during rush hour traffic.

Vin Morreale, Jr.

In the great playground of life, you are destined to be the very last to make the team. Grudgingly included only after everyone else has been picked.

Chicken Fat for the Damaged Psyche

Youth is a gourmet treat we fail to appreciate until we realize there are no second helpings.

Vin Morreale, Jr.

**Keep telling yourself
There are worse things
than being ridiculous.**

Chicken Fat for the Damaged Psyche

Isn't it odd how the least competent among us often fail in business, yet succeed in politics?

Vin Morreale, Jr.

The world you knew is gone forever. Your past; little more than rapidly fading memories. Your unappreciated present ticks away amid a thousand mosquito-like distractions, as you find yourself hurtling towards a sad future of increasing irrelevance.

Too soon, you will simply disappear. And almost no one will notice.

Regret is easy.

Pulling yourself up afterwards

is the real challenge.

Vin Morreale, Jr.

Deep down inside, you fear that you are a fraud, undeserving and barely qualified to do any of the things you have been doing. And you pray that no one will notice.

Chicken Fat for the Damaged Psyche

Public opinion is both inaccurate and overrated. Just ask anyone.

Vin Morreale, Jr.

Admit it.

You prefer to spend most nights snuggling up to a large, gooey vat of envy and self-pity.

Chicken Fat for the Damaged Psyche

The good news is you woke up this morning! The bad news is that you now have one less day to live.

Vin Morreale, Jr.

Throughout your life, you have shed people like sunburned skin.

Thousands of half-remembered faces pushed to irrelevance or filed under the oblivion of the disinterested past.

Some you envied, a few you loved, others guilty of caring too much...all discarded like the stale residue of unfinished drinks, their unique taste no longer worth even a memory.

Chicken Fat for the Damaged Psyche

They always say

'You live and learn'

But far more often

You crash and burn.

Vin Morreale, Jr.

Only those you let in your heart have the power to break it.

Manners are for little people with little minds, who have little to do but waste their little lives with vapid formality and stiflingly silly routines.

After all, how is a single flap of material descending from the neck supposed to indicate power or sophistication?

Or how choosing to wield a smaller fork to eat a salad prove refinement?

Vin Morreale, Jr.

The trouble with the world today is that there are too few really accomplished liars. Amateurs and politicians are weakening the artform.

Chicken Fat for the Damaged Psyche

Usually one has to study for years to achieve your particular level of incompetence.

Vin Morreale, Jr.

**You have a compulsively annoying need to always be right.
Feel free to prove me wrong.**

Of course, you could try to make sense. Rumor has it you once possessed that ability.

Vin Morreale, Jr.

Who knows?

Maybe someday you will be able to grow into that ego of yours.

Chicken Fat for the Damaged Psyche

Ashes to ashes

Dust to dust

Politicians are asses

One should always distrust

Vin Morreale, Jr.

Do you ever wonder why you never wonder anymore?

Don't bother looking for Happiness. You are still working through Anxiety...Boredom... Contempt... and Disillusion, so it will be a long time before you get to the H's.

Vin Morreale, Jr.

You shouldn't take compliments too seriously. Remember how much your parents praised you when you first learned to use the potty.

If it wasn't for gravity, all our wrinkles would sag upwards instead of down. Imagine how silly would grandma look then?

Vin Morreale, Jr.

Most people like to consider themselves experts on topics where expertise is meaningless.

Nations, religions, ideologues, political parties and individual fanatics all sacrifice any intellectual or moral standing they may have, once they rationalize contempt for others.

Vin Morreale, Jr.

Try not to picture what your parents had to do to make you.

Chicken Fat for the Damaged Psyche

**There will be difficulties in life.
No getting around that.**

You will be challenged, rejected, ridiculed, overlooked, overwhelmed, stressed and maybe even spat upon from time to time.

And the same holds true for anyone who has ever had an opinion.

Vin Morreale, Jr.

It is far easier to snipe from the sidelines, than committing to one side or other, and making your stand on the field of battle.

Chicken Fat for the Damaged Psyche

The glory of war lives only in victory chants, faded memories, and the eyes of those who have never tasted the anguish of battle.

Sadly, war is as natural to our species as hunger. And like hunger it can never be satisfied for long.

Vin Morreale, Jr.

We become officially tedious the day we decide to talk more than we listen.

Chicken Fat for the Damaged Psyche

**You are completely lost.
You just don't know it yet.**

Vin Morreale, Jr.

Nothing is so joyous as the first blush of true love, the gradual sharing of dreams, and the soft whispered promises of forever. But that is a thrill meant for others. Not you.

Chicken Fat for the Damaged Psyche

If they ever give an award for shallowness and self-absorption, you would be a shoo- in.

Vin Morreale, Jr.

Consider the irresistible allure of negative morality. Each compromise makes the next that much easier to rationalize. Each sin feeds another. Each betrayal becomes less shaming. Each temptation demands a further slide into the abyss. Until God sighs, and even the good man no longer recognizes how far he has fallen.

Chicken Fat for the Damaged Psyche

**Some people just don't deserve to reproduce.
Answer honestly. Would your own children put you in this category?**

Vin Morreale, Jr.

Everyone tells you to stop and smell the roses.
They never mention the thorns, fungal spores, pesticides and tiny insects that can fly right up your nose.

Chicken Fat for the Damaged Psyche

You are long past the age of being kissed with delight.

Vin Morreale, Jr.

We are all just one blush, one shred of dignity, and a few million damaged brain cells away from appearing on the next reality television show.

Chicken Fat for the Damaged Psyche

What if everything you trusted, everything you believed in, everything you built your entire life around... was nothing more than a haphazard quilt of comforting semi-truths spun by equally frightened and inept people, who just wanted some soothing fiction to make them feel better?

Would you want to know?

Or rather, do you want to know?

Vin Morreale, Jr.

You have lost any semblance of spontaneity. And even now are wondering whether you can schedule a few moments to regain it.

History is a cruel joke. We reward brutality with fame and grant the most inhuman figures immortality.

If we passed a law that any person who deserved to be remembered must never have been responsible for someone else's death, our history books would be twenty pages long.

Vin Morreale, Jr.

Most people are too polite to tell you that you have something really disgusting hanging from your nose. Have you checked a mirror recently?

Calculus is to ostriches as rules are to teenagers – totally incomprehensible.

Vin Morreale, Jr.

Return to the home of your childhood, and you will find that everything feels the same, but you. They are faded and worn to be sure, yet all the familiar pieces mesh perfectly in your absence. Over the years, you have grown too many new angles and broadened in areas beyond the narrow space once reserved for you. No matter how desperately you try, you no longer fit comfortably in this interlocking world.

How sad for you.

Chicken Fat for the Damaged Psyche

Nothing written is 100% true.

Including that.

Vin Morreale, Jr.

There are more people who consider you a complete waste of biomass than you care to admit.

Chicken Fat for the Damaged Psyche

We create stories to explain away the random brutality and arbitrary injustice of life. And we cling so fiercely to those stories that we often use them to bludgeon and brutalize others.

Vin Morreale, Jr.

Every day

In every way

We are that much closer

To decay

Underachievers hate overachievers.

Overachievers have poorly disguised contempt for underachievers.

And nobody ever considers themselves just an 'achiever.'

Vin Morreale, Jr.

Forget looks and personality. Few things makes you more attractive to the opposite sex than being an uncaring jerk with too much money.

Chicken Fat for the Damaged Psyche

We like to think of ourselves as the center of the universe.

If we were, we would be grabbed and crushed by immense gravities, sucked into a massive black hole, or incinerated by the heat and radiation of a thousand suns.

Maybe it's better to be an outsider.

Vin Morreale, Jr.

Have you ever felt like toilet paper on the rump of humanity?

Despite its tremendous promise, the earliest effect of the Internet was to introduce the term 'Lolita' to millions of people who will never read Nabokov.

Vin Morreale, Jr.

If, as the book claims, "Everything You Need To Know You Learned In Kindergarten…" consider how many years are wasted on continuing education.

Chicken Fat for the Damaged Psyche

A damaged heart.
A weary soul.
A weak and frightened inner child.
Is that what they left you?
Or was it all that remained
after they left?

Vin Morreale, Jr.

We are all ascending a long steep stairway of our own mistakes. Each day we choose whether to continue moving upward on it... Or to turn and throw ourselves back down it in despair.

More than fifty people died while you read this sentence.

Good people. People with dreams and hopes and fears. People who loved and were loved, who will be greatly missed by their families.

But they're dead...so you might as well turn the page.

Vin Morreale, Jr.

Logic is little more than cancer of the imagination.

**Without realizing it,
you have become one of those
comical dolts who mutter 'where
did the time go?'**

**To younger observers, the answer
is obvious. It is etched in the
deepening furrows of your face,
recorded in the sagging of your
neck, the upward migration of
your forehead, and the leeching of
pigment from your hair.**

Vin Morreale, Jr.

You are a master of the fine art of self-humiliation.

Chicken Fat for the Damaged Psyche

The human condition is merely the midnight noise of crickets.

Vin Morreale, Jr.

Each individual plea lost in that vast chirping symphony of complaints, excuses, sorrows and supplications.

'Notice me!' we cry. Yet how is it possible to distinguish one lone voice amid the never-ending lament of an entire self-pitying species?

Chicken Fat for the Damaged Psyche

There's no business like show business.

Except maybe prostitution, gambling or organized crime.

Your body is designed to achieve optimal health by the age of 27.

After that, you have more cells dying off than rejuvenating. Your bones and tissue grow brittle, and you can lose up to 2% of your lung capacity each year that follows.

I don't have the heart to tell you all the rest of what happens as you enter your 'Golden Years.'

There should be a special place in hell for the ones who first came up with the ideas for the speed bump, commercials in movie theaters and the male thong.

Vin Morreale, Jr.

**Most people have no idea that something is killing them until it is much too late.
And how are you feeling today?**

Think about all the people who needed you to be there for them, to say a kind word, or simply to acknowledge their existence with a phone call, a visit or even a text. But I'm sure you were much too busy to bother.

Vin Morreale, Jr.

The simple question "What if?" fills scientific journals, TV shows and divorce courts.

Why is it that as we build into our machines a deeper approximation of human thought, we seem to be systematically losing that same ability in ourselves?

Vin Morreale, Jr.

Every plant you eat crawls up out of the dirt, fertilized by decaying life, foul chemicals, or noxious substances passed through an animal's bowels.

Either that, or you devour the flesh of a creature who has digested these same things before being torn apart.

Something to think about while you wait to order at that fancy restaurant.

Chicken Fat for the Damaged Psyche

Vanity is our cruelest addiction.

Vin Morreale, Jr.

You have no problem telling others exactly how things should be done, as long as you can avoid actually doing anything yourself.

Advice is easy. Participation takes more than you are willing to give.

Chicken Fat for the Damaged Psyche

Clear your mind long enough to consider how silly the act of kissing actually looks.

Vin Morreale, Jr.

One look at you and the fiercest cannibal would go vegetarian.

Chicken Fat for the Damaged Psyche

**Why is it that those who hate what they do always seem to make up sufficient rationalizations to keep doing what they hate?
Then taking every opportunity to brag or moan about it?**

Vin Morreale, Jr.

You regularly equate cynicism with intelligence and substitute accomplishment with avoidance. Yet somehow blame life itself for being unkind to you.

Chicken Fat for the Damaged Psyche

Children instinctively enjoy the world around them. Adults squabble over every little piece of it. By this, we determine they have matured.

Vin Morreale, Jr.

Is there one thing you have done today that will be remembered twenty years from now?

Chicken Fat for the Damaged Psyche

Truth hardly matters to those who seek a reason to hate.

Vin Morreale, Jr.

Somewhere along the line, you crossed the tragic chasm of frowning more than you smile. Sadly, everyone noticed this but you.

Chicken Fat for the Damaged Psyche

Death makes you competent. Until that happens, you will always be at risk of discovery.

Vin Morreale, Jr.

If you steal as a child, you are called troubled. If you steal as an adult, you are called a thief. If you steal as a career, you are called a politician.

Chicken Fat for the Damaged Psyche

By the age of ten, you lost the ability to live in the moment.

From that point on, you began spending more of your life planning for a fictional tomorrow than learning from your embarrassing past.

Vin Morreale, Jr.

Does everyone feel trapped within their own lives? Or is it just those foolish few who are not afraid to notice?

You spent money on this book, instead of saving for retirement, investing in your education or helping to feed a starving child. Wise choice.

Vin Morreale, Jr.

Our current school system emphasizes self-esteem over traditional learning disciplines.

Al Capone and Osama bin Laden never had self-esteem problems.

Abraham Lincoln, Albert Einstein and Thomas Edison did.

Chicken Fat for the Damaged Psyche

We all know that deep down, in the darkened corners and silent shadows of your soul...

...you really can't be trusted.

Vin Morreale, Jr.

We start out life

Light and shiny

A bright illuminated soul

But soon we darken

Then surrender

To our innermost black hole

Chicken Fat for the Damaged Psyche

You may as well give up.

Nobody will even notice.

Vin Morreale, Jr.

**Realize how bizarre
the concept of professional sports really is.**

**You pay huge sums for others
to play games you want to play, because
they are so much better
at it than you will ever be.**

**It is more comfortable for you
to sit back and let them enjoy themselves,
than to actually let yourself be
part of the fun.**

Beauty is only skin deep.
Money can't buy happiness.
All things come to those who wait.
Then again, what if all those sayings are wrong?

Vin Morreale, Jr.

Have you ever looked in a full length mirror and realized how truly silly the human body looks? Especially yours?

Chicken Fat for the Damaged Psyche

You share more than 90% of your genes with worms and insects. And 99.99% with Adolph Hitler, Charles Manson, Saddam Hussein and Jeffrey Dahmer.

Vin Morreale, Jr.

With every year that passes, you lose twelve months of irretrievable possibilities.

Chicken Fat for the Damaged Psyche

Greedy and vindictive people don't have to be smart. They don't have to be right. They don't even have to be justified.

They just need a lawyer, and those replicate as quickly as any other virus.

Vin Morreale, Jr.

You smile at babies, but quickly turn your eyes from the eldery. As if childhood is humorous and impending mortality contagious.

Chicken Fat for the Damaged Psyche

Flattery...though pleasing to the taste...is nothing more than a sweet cocktail of lies, distilled by jealousy and aged by resentment.

Vin Morreale, Jr.

There is a unique flexibility to fatherhood. In one child's lifetime, you will become the center of their universe; a font of giggling delight; a superhero; a safe haven with hugs; an example of strength, integrity and bad Jokes; a teacher, disciplinarian and encourager; the wallet; a driver; their biggest fan, a growing annoyance, a petty tyrant and a complete embarrassment; a clueless dolt; an enemy to be escaped; that sad voice on the phone; a holiday obligation; a place to go for emergency cash and occasional advice; and, if fortunate, a friend; an indulgent babysitter; and soon, an object of pity; an increasing burden; a growing cause for concern; and one day, little more than a bittersweet memory... all over the course of three to seven wonderful, but rapidly disappearing decades.

Breathing and eating are actually toxic to the body. Every breath you take, every meal you eat has a small, corrosive effect that will kill you over time.

Vin Morreale, Jr.

One's reputation is far too important to be kept spotless.

Too often, you use the term 'tolerance' as an excuse for inaction. A cowardly way to avoid the discomfort of asking people to do their best.

Vin Morreale, Jr.

There will never be a lack of fanatics who believe the only way to honor their God is to senselessly slaughter as many of his children as possible. And now they have their eyes on you.

Chicken Fat for the Damaged Psyche

There is a cure for intelligence.

It is called 'internet trolling.'

Vin Morreale, Jr.

Do we ever really live up to our true potential? And if we did, would our 'potential' then increase, so we then face even more we are asked to live up to?

Chicken Fat for the Damaged Psyche

Life is a high-speed chase. We careen between the fast lane of quickly dissipating rapture and off-ramps of utter despair. Which road are you on today?

Vin Morreale, Jr.

If only people realized that added volume and childish insults never make an argument more convincing.

Chicken Fat for the Damaged Psyche

Sure, you do the occasional favor and charitable thing. But you constantly keep track of each one, instead of offering them freely. Aren't you special?

Vin Morreale, Jr.

Good intentions always carry their own punishment.

Chicken Fat for the Damaged Psyche

You know that nothing of consequence has ever been accomplished, except by those who suffered the bitter slap of fear, swallowed hard, then dared it to stop them.

Still you find it so much easier to envy them than to mirror their courage.

Vin Morreale, Jr.

Some believe that everything you are, everything you think and everything you feel is merely the random interplay of chemicals and bioelectricity. Even reading this sentence is nothing more than the discharge of neural impulses, sparked by a sloshing of proteins within your brain. One day soon, those chemicals will leak out, the electrical triggers will cease to fire, and your entire consciousness will simply evaporate into nothingness.

Let's hope they're wrong.

There are only three types of people in the world: the tragic the ridiculous and the self-deluded.
In you, they come dangerously close to overlapping.

Vin Morreale, Jr.

Every breath you take contains molecules ripped from the lungs and bodies of many strangers who are long dead.

Chicken Fat for the Damaged Psyche

**There will never be enough time to do everything you were destined to do.
And even if there was,
you know you would find some foolish way to keep putting it off.
So why do anything?**

Vin Morreale, Jr.

Don't for a moment think that suicide is the answer. With your luck, there will be far more pain and suffering on the other side.

Chicken Fat for the Damaged Psyche

No matter how old, accomplished, or respectable we become, there will always be those who only remember the really stupid things we did in high school.

Vin Morreale, Jr.

No sense crying to the heavens.

They've heard it all before.

Chicken Fat for the Damaged Psyche

Maybe our eyes are on the front of our face for a reason...

...so we never see how ridiculous we look most of the time.

Vin Morreale, Jr.

If only you knew how often your dearest and most trusted love imagines the face of another during your most intimate moments. That secret smile of sleep hiding other arms that silently steal your place in your lover's dreams.

Chicken Fat for the Damaged Psyche

On any given day, most people in the world are hopelessly boring and somehow fail to realize it. Are you sure you're not one of them?

Vin Morreale, Jr.

Children are always noticed.

As you age, your invisibility factor increases. One day, you will walk down the street and realize that at least half the people you pass are substantially younger than you. And that percentage only grows with each passing year, until you become little more than a shadow to virtually everyone who passes you by.

Chicken Fat for the Damaged Psyche

You are fooling no one.

Vin Morreale, Jr.

We are only allotted a certain number of breaths in this lifetime. A limited number of heartbeats.

We can never know the exact count, but it will likely be millions less than we expect. And billions less than we hope for.

Perhaps the best we can hope for is that nobody realizes how barely competent we really are.

Vin Morreale, Jr.

Evil exists as mankind's closest companion.

We may try to deny its hypnotic hold on us. Yet, why else do we choose as entertainment an orgy of books, movies and reality shows based on murder, betrayal and the sudden extinguishing of innocent life?

Chicken Fat for the Damaged Psyche

**The good things you do in life are mostly forgettable to everyone but yourself.
The bad things stick to your reputation like cement.**

Vin Morreale, Jr.

It's a shame you never learned from your mistakes or noticed how far out of whack your priorities have proven to be.

Chicken Fat for the Damaged Psyche

Virtues are seldom appreciated. Especially by those who have tossed theirs aside.

Vin Morreale, Jr.

Remember all those people you used to make fun of behind their backs? How good is your hearing these days?

Why are women who go after younger men called cougars, while men who go after younger women are called...well, men?

Vin Morreale, Jr.

If you can't giggle during sex, why bother?

Chicken Fat for the Damaged Psyche

It is easier to believe the stories we are told, than stare unblinking at the harsh truth with all its unmasked guilt and implications.

Vin Morreale, Jr.

Why is it that so many who once screamed "Make love, not war" happily give medals to soldiers and jail terms to hookers?

Chicken Fat for the Damaged Psyche

The night is a long, dark hall seeped with shadows of doubt. We are at most tiny creatures cowering in the corner, trying so hard not to hear our own desperate breaths.

Vin Morreale, Jr.

Today's forecast: haughty with a high chance of condescension. Tomorrow will be rude with a twenty percent probability of sarcasm.

Chicken Fat for the Damaged Psyche

There is always a light at the end of the tunnel. Although that may mean another train is heading straight towards you.

Vin Morreale, Jr.

**We all behave like walking movies, replaying the filtered, fractured and fictionalized chaos of our past. Yet somehow thinking we are real. We are in control. At least until our last reel unspools. Then it's lights out. Curtain closed.
And what the hell happened?**

Chicken Fat for the Damaged Psyche

You have let the Inner Critic of your past ambush the amazing potential of your Future Dreamer.

Vin Morreale, Jr.

When exactly did the rules of disagreement and debate turn into degrade, destroy and disrespect?

Chicken Fat for the Damaged Psyche

Did you ever wonder if crabs feel bad about having their name associated with itchy crotches and negative people like you?

Vin Morreale, Jr.

You mourn the obstacles in life, knowing the easy path offers no time for reflection. No reason for change. No opportunity for growth.

Corruption lies in numbers

We behave like fire, that most elemental blessing to early man. In small amounts, it warms, protects, inspires, sterilizes and enlightens. Yet as it grows, it risks destructiveness, yearning to escape beyond controllable bounds; free to char, torture and consume all in its path. So too are we, righteous as individuals, but conscienceless in a crowd. The anonymity of the mob loosens our inner fiends, so that even shared horrors become a rite of membership. How else to explain corporate ethics, crooked charities or mass exhortations to kill in the name of religion?

Vin Morreale, Jr.

Some people consider you as appealing as antique mayonnaise.

Chicken Fat for the Damaged Psyche

Keep telling yourself, 'It is better to have loved and lost than never to have loved at all.' We call that the loser's mantra.

Vin Morreale, Jr.

Beware the creeping crush of night
The sad soft whisper, 'no return'
That dark seductress' gentle bite
Or talons, teeth and tears that burn
Oh, promised vacuum's blinded eye
Relief from anguish evermore
Lulled to sleep, this darkened sky
No time. No thought. No I. No more
No time. No thought. No I
No...

Chicken Fat for the Damaged Psyche

You have picked on, ignored, ridiculed, criticized, gossiped about, or treated someone cruelly for no other reason than to impress someone else.

Vin Morreale, Jr.

Every father dreams of giving birth to his own reflection in manner, interests and ambitions. And every father is secretly let down when his son begins to develop his own ideas.

Chicken Fat for the Damaged Psyche

Apathy, inertia, lack of courage or voluntary distraction make you complicit in every evil perpetrated on your fellow man.

Vin Morreale, Jr.

You care in the collective but feel nothing for the personal.

Chicken Fat for the Damaged Psyche

Your self-image is many dimensions removed from reality.

Vin Morreale, Jr.

You will seek out love

your entire life.

Until you eventually go senile.

Then you will probably

fall in love with a toaster.

Chicken Fat for the Damaged Psyche

Worry is a thief and a liar. It steals your enjoyment of each precious moment and cons you with a hundred horrible futures that will never happen.

Vin Morreale, Jr.

It is easy to be the one nobody expects anything from. All you have to do is fail… and fail consistently.

Chicken Fat for the Damaged Psyche

You have finished this book.
Now what are you going
To do with your life?

About the Authors

NEVADA BLUE PICCOLETTI, or 'Nev' to her friends, is a Private Investigator and ex-cop in Louisville, Kentucky, who likes to write depressing humor to help her through various cases involving kidnapping, corruption and murder.

VIN MORREALE, JR. is the award-winning screenwriter, playwright and author who chronicles her adventures in the SOUTHERN CROSS series. His diverse body of work ranges from children's books and screen comedy to horror novels, business writing, historical romance, stage musicals and theology.

You can find more at AcademyArtsPress.com.

www.ingramcontent.com/pod-product-compliance
Lightning Source LLC
Chambersburg PA
CBHW081103080526
44587CB00021B/3436